靜思精舍惜物造福的智慧故事④

慈悲
福慧床的故事

總策劃 / 靜思書軒

The Wisdom of Cherishing and Sowing Blessings
at the Jing Si Abode (4)
Compassion: The Story of the Jing Si Multipurpose Folding Bed

下課回家後，小慈興奮的跟媽媽說：「媽媽，今天我們去靜思書軒看書的時候，我發現有個很酷的東西喔！」

　　媽媽說：「很酷的東西？我來猜猜看，是⋯⋯立體書？」

小慈說：「不是，是家具類的物品。」

媽媽說：「家具類？讓我想想……」

When Xiao-Ci came home from school, she immediately ran to her mother and said excitedly, "Mom! Today, when we went to the Jing Si Bookstore, I saw something really cool!"

Xiao-Ci's mother said, "Something cool? Let me guess... was it a pop-up book?"

Xiao-Ci said, "No, it was a type of furniture."

Xiao-Ci's mother said, "Furniture? Let me think..."

「公布答案！是『福慧床』，可以像變形金剛那樣，變來變去！一開始是一個扁扁的正方形，拉開一半後，可以變成椅子，全部拉開之後，還可以變成一張可以睡覺的床。」小慈興奮的說。

媽媽一邊查資料，一邊對小慈說：「『福慧床』的背後有精彩的故事，我來告訴你喔。」

"I'll tell you! It was the Jing Si Multipurpose Folding Bed! It can be folded and transformed, just like a Transformer! It started out folded up in a small square. When you partially unfold it, it becomes a chair, and then when you unfold it all the way, it turns into a bed you can sleep on!" Xiao-Ci said excitedly.

Xiao-Ci's mother looked up more information on the folding bed, and said to Xiao-Ci, "Let me tell you the story of the Jing Si Multipurpose Folding Bed! It's actually very interesting!"

2010年，巴基斯坦發生了一場嚴重的水災，不但淹沒五分之一的國土面積，更有兩千萬人流離失所。災民們不僅失去家園，連休息安頓的地方都沒有，只能在冰冷泥濘的地上等待救援。

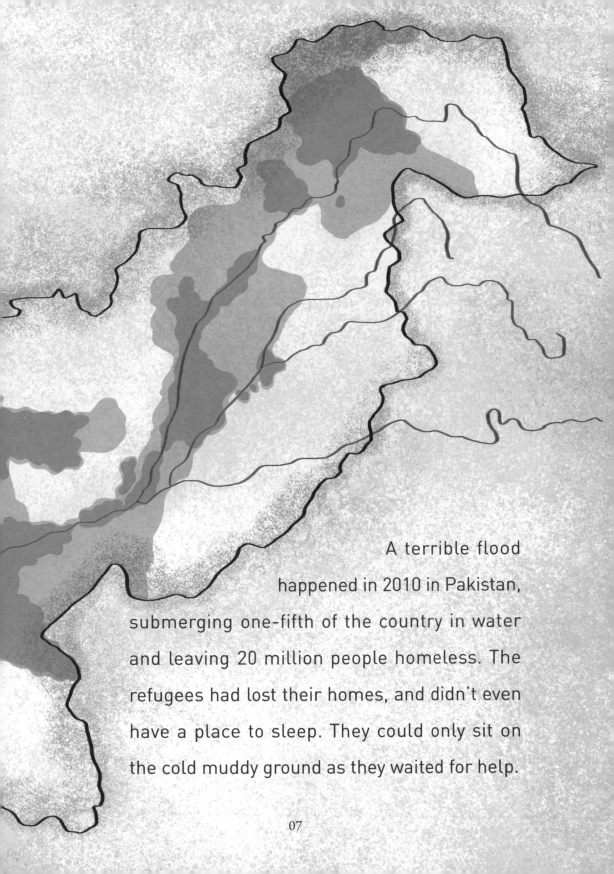

A terrible flood happened in 2010 in Pakistan, submerging one-fifth of the country in water and leaving 20 million people homeless. The refugees had lost their homes, and didn't even have a place to sleep. They could only sit on the cold muddy ground as they waited for help.

證嚴上人看到了新聞報導中，剛出生的女嬰夏娜睡在一個沒有遮蔽的棚子裡，小小的身軀就躺在地上。上人說：「受災居民很苦，再讓他們睡在地上的積水中，情何以堪。」上人的內心非常著急，希望大家一起幫忙想想辦法。

Dharma Master Cheng Yen saw on the news a newly-born baby named Shana, who could only sleep under a canopy. Her tiny body was curled up on the ground. Dharma Master Cheng Yen said, "The refugees are already suffering, but now they must sleep in the water and mud. This is terrible!" Dharma Master Cheng Yen, deeply worried, asked everyone to think of a solution.

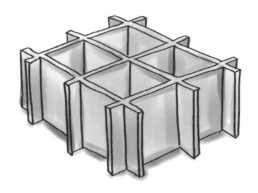

　　很快的，一群志工們設計出「簡易組合式睡床」，材質是塑膠瓦楞板，重量很輕，一個人就可以輕鬆搬運，床架用井字交叉組成，每條床架也有凹槽，可以支撐重物。隔年，慈濟就開始把這組睡床送到巴基斯坦的災區，緊急賑災。

A group of volunteers quickly designed a bed that could be easily assembled. It was made of plastic corrugated boards, which made it very lightweight; one person could easily carry it alone. The frame of the bed, made of criss-crossing struts, had grooves that could be used to hold things up. Tzu Chi started delivering the beds to the affected parts of Pakistan the next year.

　　志工還特地製作一張嬰兒床，送給當時已經四個月大的小夏娜。不過，後來發現切割後的瓦楞板邊緣鋒利，拆卸時容易割傷手等問題，於是蔡思一師兄開始接手進行改良工作。

The volunteers even made a special baby bed for Shana, who was four months old at the time. However, they found that the corrugated boards often had sharp edges, which sometimes cut the hands of the people building or taking apart the beds. As a result, Jing Si's Brother Marshall Siao started redesigning the bed.

第一代「福慧床」誕生了，以食品級PP塑膠材質打造床板，方便清潔；其中最具巧思的地方是在底板和側板開了許多洞，這些洞不僅可以在多變的災區環境裡更加便利，如遇積水時讓水流過去，床組也不易遇水遭致損毀，還可以減輕床組的重量。

This led to the creation of the first-generation Jing Si Multipurpose Folding Bed. The boards were made with food-grade polypropylene plastic, which made it easy to clean. Holes were cleverly added to the base board and side boards, which meant water in the

flooded areas would simply flow away through the bed, and the bed itself would not be damaged by water. The holes also made the bed lighter.

　　從研發過程中的實心床板改為洞洞床板，不僅更通風，散熱功能更好，而且重量減輕了，搬運時也更加輕巧便利，高度下降了，攤平時也更加穩固。

　　經過不斷改善，第二代更加成熟的「福慧床」終於問世了，同時還能組裝蚊帳，發揮更全面性的功能。

Later, holes were added to the bed board to improve ventilation and keep the user cool. It also made the bed even lighter and easier to move. Furthermore, the height of the bed was lowered to make it more stable when unfolded.

Constant improvements were made until an even better, second-generation of Jing Si Multipurpose Folding Bed was created. Mosquito nets can even be attached to this version of the bed, giving it even more features.

福慧床不僅可承重150公斤，尺寸和強度都符合單人床的標準，摺疊後幾乎只有一只皮箱的大小，不管是運送或收納，都十分圓滿。一個標準貨櫃可以裝進五百張福慧床，非常節省空間！

　　The Jing Si Multipurpose Folding Bed can carry up to 150 kilograms, and its size and sturdiness are all very suitable for a single person bed. It's around the size of a suitcase when folded up, making it easy to carry and store. A standard-sized shipping container can hold five hundred Jing Si Multipurpose Folding Beds!

2013年，菲律賓遭受海燕颱風的侵襲，一家都是菲律賓僑胞也是慈濟人的蔡思一，哥哥、姊姊和妹妹全部回去菲律賓幫忙賑災，他獨自留守花蓮，幫忙檢視才剛上市不久的「福慧床」運送到菲律賓的流程，「福慧床」可以說是賑災時最強大的後盾。

In 2013, the Philippines was struck by Typhoon Haiyan. Marshall Siao's family are from the Philippines, so his brother and two sisters all returned to the Philippines to help the affected people. But Marshall stayed in Hualien to supervise the Jing Si Multipurpose Folding Beds being sent to the Philippines.

災民們樂天的個性，將「福慧床」的功能發揮到極致。白天的時候，「福慧床」可以當成醫師的臨時病床看診，或是摺成椅子，大家可以聚在一起，也陪伴孩子。

The people affected by the typhoon, with their easy-going nature, made full use of the Jing Si Multipurpose Folding Bed 's various functions. In the daytime, patients could lie on the beds for doctors to examine them. They could also be folded into chairs, for people and families to sit on together.

到了晚上，可以把「福慧床」全部攤平，兩、三張床併排，一家人就可以在星空下乘著些許的涼風，安安穩穩的休憩入睡。

At night, the Jing Si Multipurpose Folding Beds would be unfolded and placed side-by-side, and whole families would be able to sleep soundly under the stars.

「福慧床」推出後成為各地賑災的最佳幫手，更得到了許多國際知名的設計大獎。2015年「淨斯多功能福慧床」在「匹茲堡國際發明展」中獲得兩項金牌。2016年，主辦單位更特別頒發「發明教育貢獻獎」給證嚴上人。

The Jing Si Multipurpose Folding Bed became one of the best tools for disaster relief, and has won many design awards around the world. In 2015, the Jing Si Multipurpose Folding Bed won two gold medals at the Invention and New Product Exposition (INPEX) in Pittsburgh; in 2016, the organizers also awarded Dharma Master Cheng Yen with the Invention Educational Award.

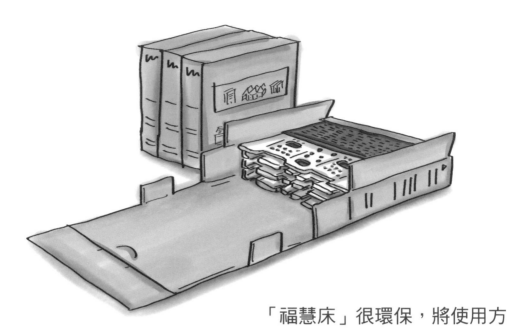

「福慧床」很環保，將使用方法直接印在紙盒上，不但可減少印製說明書的紙張，更將包裝的紙板設計成簡易床墊，完全不浪費，託運時紙盒下面有兩個可愛的小輪子，是由回收紙捲製作而成。

To help protect the environment, the instructions for the Jing Si Multipurpose Folding Bed are printed directly on the cardboard box, so no extra paper is wasted. The cardboard box can also be turned into a make-shift mattress so that it's not wasted. There are even two cute little wheels made from recycled cardboard that people can use to roll the bed around in the box.

「媽媽，我覺得『福慧床』這名字很優雅，為什麼叫做『福慧床』呢？」小慈問。

　　「這是好問題。由於上人經常勉勵慈濟人『福慧雙修』，『福慧床』便以此為名。」媽媽溫柔的說。

"Mom, the name of the Jing Si Multipurpose Folding Bed in Chinese is 'Fu Hui.' Why is it called 'Fu Hui?'" Xiao-Ci asked.

"That's a good question. It's because Dharma Master Cheng Yen often teaches Tzu Chi members, 'fu hui shuang xiu,' which means 'to cultivate both blessings and wisdom.' That's what the folding bed is named after," Xiao-Ci's mother said gently.

「小慈，你知道嗎？『福慧床』完成後，蔡師兄還設計了環保蚊帳，材質輕便，容易清洗，可以隨身攜帶，除了防蚊和防蟲，還可以防毒蛇。更重要的是利用環保回收材質來製作。」媽媽說。

"Xiao-Ci, do you know? After Brother Marshall Siao designed the folding bed, he also designed environmentally-friendly mosquito nets. They're lightweight and easy to clean! They protect against mosquitoes and other bugs, as well as poisonous snakes! And the most important thing is that they're made of recycled materials," Xiao-Ci's mother said.

「上人看到剛出生的夏娜在災區受苦受難，慈悲心油然生起，弟子們將這份慈悲心化作行動，共知、共識、共行，一邊修行志業，一邊參與解決世界所發生的苦難。」媽媽很感性地為故事畫下一個溫暖的結局。

"Dharma Master Cheng Yen felt for the newborn Shana when she saw her suffering. Her disciples turned this

compassion into action by building consensus, sharing knowledge, and working together. This meant they could cultivate themselves while helping to solve problems around the world," Xiao-Ci's mother said emotionally as she brought the story to its end.

「我也覺得很感動，原來『福慧床』背後有這麼感人的故事。」媽媽說。

「明天我要去學校跟班上的同學分享這個故事！」小慈開心的說。

"The Jing Si Multipurpose Folding Bed has such a touching story behind it," Xiao-Ci's mother said.

"Tomorrow, I'm going to tell my classmates at school all about the Jing Si Multipurpose Folding Bed," Xiao-Ci declared happily.

一起來認識福慧家具！
Let's Learn More about Jing Si Furniture!

看完了福慧床的故事，一起來認識福慧家具系列。除了福慧床，還有福慧桌椅、福慧隔屏，在每個地方都發光、發亮！

除了福慧床，還有福慧桌椅、福慧隔屏

福慧家具系列包含了福慧床、福慧桌椅和福慧隔屏，是從慈濟人賑災經驗中發想設計的，多功能的設計解決了救災各種情況的需求，安心又安身。平時，福慧家具因為好收納多用途的優點，非常適合空間有限的環境使用，像是家裡有客人來訪留宿、室外活動時，都能輕鬆地派上用場。

2024 年 4 月 3 日臺灣發生大地震，花蓮受損嚴重，慈濟志工在短時間內，設置好能讓災民保有隱私的福慧隔屏，也獲得災民和各國媒體的報導與肯定。

（攝影者：徐政裕）

After learning about the Jing Si Multipurpose Folding Bed, let's learn more about other pieces of Jing Si Furniture, such as The Jing Si Table, Chair, and Partition Tents.

The Jing Si Table, Chair, and Partition Tents

Jing Si Furniture includes the Jing Si Multipurpose Folding Bed as well as The Jing Si Table, Chair, and Partition Tents. They were designed by Tzu Chi volunteers based on their disaster relief experiences, and they are meant to solve many different problems in disaster areas. Jing Si Furniture is foldable and easy to store, so they are suitable for areas with limited space. For example, they can be brought out when you have guests staying over at your home, or when you have outdoor activities. A major earthquake struck Taiwan on April 3, 2024, causing severe damage in Hualien. Tzu Chi volunteers quickly set up Jing Si Partition Tents to provide privacy to people driven from their homes, which received widespread approval from affected people as well as international media reports.

On April 4, 2024, Tzu Chi volunteers continued to provide care and assistance to earthquake victims at the emergency shelter in Hua Ren Junior High School, Ji'an Township, Hualien County, where Jing Si Partition Tents and Jing Si Folding Beds had been set up. (Photo by Kun-cheng Xue)

2024 年 4 月 4 日慈濟志工在已設置福慧隔屏及鋪設福慧床的花蓮吉安鄉化仁國中避難所，持續關懷災民，提供必要協助。（攝影者：薛崑城）

福慧家具發揮大功能

不管國內或國外的賑災現場，「福慧床」和「福慧桌椅」都提供最簡潔和有力的支持與幫助。近年，「靜思閱讀書軒」在全臺灣的學校遍地開花，閱讀書軒裡的家具也都是福慧家具，除了實用的「福慧桌椅」，「福慧床」也大獲好評。不僅嘉惠學生，建立良好的閱讀習慣，並在福慧家具的擁抱之下，閱讀寫字，陪伴年輕學子開創屬於自己的繽紛未來。

Jing Si Furniture Used in Many Different Settings

Jing Si Multipurpose Folding Beds, Tables, and Chairs have been a great help in disasters area in Taiwan and abroad, providing simple yet reliable support to everyone. In recent years, Jing Si Reading Rooms have been set up at schools throughout Taiwan, and Jing Si Furniture is used in these reading rooms as well. Aside from Jing Si Tables and Chairs, the Jing Si Multipurpose Folding Bed has also been a popular choice. They help create a suitable environment for students to study and gain their knowledge, which means they will be able to have a better future.

靜思語：慈悲

把貪念轉為滿足，把滿足化作慈悲。

Transform greed into contentment,
and contentment into compassion.

《中英對照靜思小語1》│《小學生 365 靜思語》

愛心不分遠近，慈悲沒有敵對和親愛。

Love is not bound by distance;
compassion is free from aversion and passion.

《靜思語第三集》

最幸福的人生，就是能寬容與悲憫
一切眾生的人生。

A person with a generous heart and
compassion for all beings leads the most blessed life.

《中英對照靜思小語1》│《小學生 365 靜思語》

對每件事、每個人都感恩，
就能化貪心為慈悲心。

Always keep gratitude in mind and
greed shall give way to compassion.

《靜思語第三集》|《小學生 365 靜思語》

以愛待人、以慈對人，則不惹人怨，亦能結好緣。

When we treat others with love and compassion,
we will not stir up ill feelings,
and we will be able to form
good relationships with others.

《中英對照靜思小語 1》|《小學生 365 靜思語》

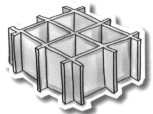

關於福慧家具

給老師和家長們更多關於福慧家具的資訊。

　　曾經獲得2014年德國紅點設計大獎（Red Dot Design Award）「最高品質獎」、2015年美國匹茲堡國際發明展「金牌」、「慈善公益特別獎」、「iENA德國紐倫堡國際發明展」「金牌獎」、「中國好設計」「優勝獎」等獎項肯定的福慧家具系列，具有好收納多用途的優點。走訪「靜思書軒」或校園裡的「靜思閱讀書軒」，都可以體驗「福慧床」、「福慧桌椅」這項智慧研發，現在仍然持續運用於許多救災現場！

　　2024年4月3日臺灣發生大地震，在花蓮的救災安置場所中，出現一排排注重被安置者隱私的「淨斯福慧環保隔屏」，隔屏內放置「福慧床」及「福慧桌椅」，可供災民和志工躺臥休息，大大獲得各國媒體的報導和讚賞。

靜思人文
JING SI CULTURE

靜思精舍惜物造福的智慧故事 4

慈悲：福慧床的故事

總 策 劃／靜思書軒
編 審／蔡思一
照片提供／靜思書軒‧慈濟基金會文史處
故 事／陳佳聖
插 圖／江長芳
美術設計／陳俐君
英 譯／ Linguitronics Co., Ltd. 萬象翻譯（股）公司（故事及主題延伸）

總 編 輯／李復民
副總編輯／鄧懿貞
特約主編／陳佳聖
封面設計／ Javick 工作室
專案企劃／蔡孟庭、盤惟心

讀書共和國出版集團 業務平台
總 經 理／李雪麗　　　　　副總經理／李復民
海外業務總監／張鑫峰　　　特販業務總監／陳綺瑩
零售資深經理／郭文弘　　　專案企劃總監／蔡孟庭
印務協理／江域平　　　　　印務主任／李孟儒

出 版／發光體文化／遠足文化事業股份有限公司
發 行／遠足文化事業股份有限公司（讀書共和國出版集團）
地 址／ 231 新北市新店區民權路 108 之 2 號 9 樓
電 話／（02）2218-1417　　　傳眞／（02）8667-1065
電子信箱／ service@bookrep.com.tw
網 址／ www.bookrep.com.tw
郵撥帳號／ 19504465 遠足文化事業股份有限公司

法律顧問／華洋法律事務所　蘇文生律師
印 製／凱林彩印股份有限公司

慈濟人文出版社
地 址／臺北市忠孝東路三段二一七巷七弄十九號一樓
電 話／（02）2898-9888
傳 眞／（02）2898-9889
網 址／ www.jingsi.org

2024 年 5 月 2 日初版一刷　　　　定 價／ 320 元
ISBN ／ 978-626-98109-6-3（精裝）　書 號／ 2IGN1008

國家圖書館出版品預行編目資料

靜思精舍惜物造福的智慧故事 . 4. 慈悲：福慧床的故事 = The wisdom of cherishing and sowing blessings at the Jing Si Abode. 4, compassion : the story of the Jing Si Multipurpose folding bed／陳佳聖故事 . -- 新北市：遠足文化事業股份有限公司發光體文化，遠足文化事業股份有限公司，2024.04
40 面；17×23 公分
中英對照
ISBN 978-626-98109-6-3（精裝）

224.515　　　　　　　　　　　113003671